Collection Management and
Development Guides, no. 4

GUIDE TO
BUDGET
ALLOCATION
FOR
INFORMATION
RESOURCES

Subcommittee on Budget Allocation
Collection Management and Development Committee
Resources Section
Association for Library Collections & Technical Services

Edward Shreeves, editor

AMERICAN LIBRARY ASSOCIATION

Chicago and London 1991

Cover and text design by Charles Bozett.
Composition by Beverly Thymes in English Times using Bestinfo.
Printed on 60-pound Heritage Antique Book, Ph-neutral stock,
and bound in 10-point Carolina cover stock by Imperial Printing
Company.

The paper used in this publication meets the minimum requirements of
American National Standard for Information Sciences--Permanence of
Paper for Printed Library Materials, ANSI Z39.48-1984. ∞

Library of Congress Cataloging-in-Publication Data

Guide to budget allocation for information resources / Subcommittee on
   Budget Allocation, Collection Management and Development Com-
   mittee, Resources Section, Association for Library Collections and
   Technical Services ; Edward Shreeves, editor.
      p.   cm.
   Includes bibliographical references.
   ISBN 0-8389-3397-1
   1. Acquisitions (Libraries).   2. Library materials--Prices.
3. Program budgeting.   4. Library finance.   I. Shreeves, Edward.
II. Association for Library Collections & Technical Services.
Collection Management and Development Committee. Subcommit-
tee on Budget Allocation.
Z689.G86   1991
025.2—dc20   91-9371
                                                     CIP

Printed in the United States of America.
95 94 93 92 91   5 4 3 2 1

Subcommittee on Budget Allocation
Collection Management and Development Committee
Resources Section
Association for Library Collections & Technical Services

Carolyn Bucknall, chair
Yvonne Chen
Gay Dannelly
Angela Lindley
Edward Shreeves, editor
Karin Wittenborg

CONTENTS

PREFACE

The Subcommittee on Budget Allocation offers this guide with the realization that it provides no more than signposts to assist those finding their way through the budgeting process. Budgets, and the budgeting context, differ so much from one library to another, not to mention among libraries of different types, that precise directions are an impossible ideal. We hope that the principles and information presented here will offer some general guidance toward the goal.

This guide represents a complete reworking of "Guidelines for the Allocation of Library Materials Budgets," published as part of the *Guidelines for Collection Development,* edited by David L. Perkins (Chicago: American Library Association, 1979). It is the fourth in a series of guides being issued by the Collection Management and Development Committee, Resources Section, Association for Library Collections & Technical Services (formerly Resources and Technical Services Division).

Thanks are due a number of people who provided advice and comments on earlier drafts. William McPheron contributed a working bibliography during a brief stint on the subcommittee at the beginning of its work. Others who offered suggestions and assistance include Jasper Schad, Gerald Hodges, Kathryn Hammell Carpenter, Bette Bohler, Bonita Bryant, and the others who offered comments at subcommittee meetings and the hearing held in 1989 at the Annual Conference in Dallas.

1. Introduction

1.1. Purpose

This guide is intended to assist librarians making information resources budget allocations by describing the character and function of the budget document, stating allocation principles, presenting an array of considerations and options for application to the local budget allocation process, and enumerating sources of information helpful to that process.

1.2. Need

Every library, regardless of size or type, allocates funds for information resources. The process of creating the budget, while varying considerably from one institution to another, has common components. This revision of the 1979 guide recognizes the need for additional guidance in budget allocation in an environment characterized by rapid economic, technological, and organizational change.

1.3. Intended audience and scope

The guide is intended to assist librarians who participate in the budget process—as library administrators, as administrators of collection development and management programs, or as librarians who practice collection development and management—in all types of libraries. While the document does not provide instructions on making a budget request or proposing expenditures to a parent agency, much that is covered is also relevant to that process.

2. The information resources budget document

Although this section speaks of the ''budget document,'' in fact, depending on purpose and audience, the budget document may take on a variety of forms during the fiscal cycle.

2.1. Purposes

The budget document simultaneously serves a multiplicity of functions, including planning, monitoring, and communication.

2.1.1.

It serves as a tool by which the person or persons responsible for collection development translate collecting priorities into a concrete form.

1

2.1.2.	It functions as a medium for requesting funds from or proposing expenditures to a funding source.
2.1.3.	It documents the amounts allocated to each subaccount (or allocation unit) and offers an explicit plan for expenditures.
2.1.4.	It communicates budget information to a variety of audiences and helps to develop support for and trust in allocation decisions.
2.1.5.	It serves as a measure for performance and a means of controlling expenditures.
2.1.6.	It acts as an historical record showing actual expenditures, including variances from the initial budget.
2.2.	**Audiences**
	The audience for the budget document will vary according to the purpose it fulfills at any given time. The content and format of the document itself may vary according to the particular audience. Possible audiences include:
2.2.1.	Members of the administration or governing body to which a library reports, such as a school official or school board, board of trustees, city manager, department head, or college president.
2.2.2.	The library administration, including the director and other administrative officers, along with appropriate internal advisory councils or committees.
2.2.3.	Selection officers, such as bibliographers, branch heads, members of a selection committee, faculty members, and others with authority and responsibility for spending funds.
2.2.4.	Units within and outside the library that are involved in the acquisitions process or in maintaining accounting records for information resources funds.
2.2.5.	Outside groups with an advisory relationship to the library (such as faculty library committees, public library advisory boards, school curriculum committees) and library users generally.
2.3.	**General characteristics of an effective budget document**
2.3.1.	The format is usually tabular, a two-dimensional matrix organized on one axis according to allocation unit and on the other axis according to the fiscal category or activity being

presented. The specifics will vary widely from library to library, and may be affected by the accounting system used by the individual library or its parent institution.

2.3.1.1.   Allocation units

Basic allocation units may be organized into groups, arranged hierarchically, or simply listed; they may be presented first in summary form, then with greater detail, in either a different part of the same document or in a different document.

2.3.1.2.   Fiscal categories

In addition to the allocation for the current year, the budget document may also show funds and encumbrances brought forward from the previous year, additional income and deductions, increases or decreases in the base allocation, and similar information. Often the budget document in some version contains comparative figures showing allocations and/or expenditures for the current year and one or more previous years.

2.3.2.   Recommended features of effective budget documents

2.3.2.1.   Information should be presented clearly enough that a layperson can understand the document without assistance.

2.3.2.2.   Technical terminology, when used at all, should be used in accordance with accepted standards.

2.3.2.3.   Abbreviations should be used only when they will be commonly understood by intended audiences.

2.3.2.4.   Footnotes may be used to amplify data that departs from the expected or customary.

2.3.2.5.   Textual material, graphs, or charts may be added to accompany tables as appropriate for the intended audience.

2.4.   Preparation

2.4.1.   Budget documents are usually prepared by the librarian with administrative responsibility for collection development (collection development officer, director, etc.) or by a library committee with selection responsibilities.

2.4.2.   Participation by those affected in the budget preparation process helps ensure its successful implementation and outcome. The Resources and Technical Services Division's publication *Guide to Writing a Bibliographer's Manual* (published by the American Library Association in 1987) discusses these activities in detail.

2.4.3.   Both the data used in preparation of the budget document and the procedures by which that data is transformed into allocations should undergo regular review to ensure that they meet the goals of the library.

2.4.4.   Activities related to the preparation, review, and approval of the budget should begin early enough to allow for timely issuance of the budget document.

3.   **Allocation principles**

This section describes the basic underlying assumptions guiding the allocation process.

3.1.   Allocations should further institutional objectives as stated in:
1.   the goals of the parent agency
2.   the mission and goals of the library
3.   the collection development policy
4.   priorities set in the planning process.

3.2.   The budget document and the allocation process should engender confidence on both the fiscal and political level.

3.2.1.   Allocations should present a realistic plan of expenditures.

3.2.2.   Allocations should take political pressures into account and minimize vulnerability to special interests seeking exceptional treatment.

3.2.3.   Allocations should be based on agreed upon criteria consistently applied to all allocations in similar categories.

3.2.4.   In order to promote acceptance, changes in allocation methods should be implemented only after consultation.

3.3.   Funds should be allocated by librarians or designated representatives of the library staff. Librarians or their representatives are in a position to gather the information needed to develop allocation plans and to evaluate the demands made on information resources in light of institutional goals.

3.4.   The allocation process should encourage broad participation, especially of library selectors with respect to their
specific areas of collection responsibility. Activities that
involve participation include:
1.   information gathering
2.   budget proposals
3.   allocation review
4.   evaluation of budget as actually expended.

3.5.   Information about the budget should be publicized to staff
and users so that there is general understanding of the
funding structure, the amounts allocated to major areas, and
the factors leading to this particular division of funds.

3.6.   The budget should be flexible enough to provide for
economic contingencies or purchase opportunities.

3.7.   Funds must be reserved at the outset for ongoing commitments (such as serials).

4.   **The allocation process: Planning, preparation, and
review**
This section brings the activities associated with the
allocation process from the planning to the documentation
stage. Section 5 and the Appendix describe appropriate tools
and information sources relating to these activities.

4.1.   **Planning**

4.1.1.   Schedule activities to allow for timely issuance of the
budget document.

4.1.2.   Assemble necessary information for planning purposes.

4.1.3.   Analyze needs and set priorities.

4.2.   **Forecasting and projecting**

4.2.1.   Assemble information on costs of continuing obligations
(such as serials and approval plans) from the preceding year
and forecast fluctuations for the coming year.

4.2.1.1.   This activity will involve an analysis of economic conditions, such as inflation, recession, and currency exchange
rates, as they affect ongoing commitments.

4.2.1.2.   As expenditures for continuing obligations are made during

5

the year, forecasted rates can be tested against actual rates and the model revised as desired.

4.2.2. Assemble information with regard to non-continuing costs for previous years and use it to forecast anticipated costs by allocation unit.

4.3. **Structuring the budget: Choice of allocation units**

4.3.1. Budgets are structured according to the allocation units selected. Typically, several allocation units are selected for inclusion in a single budget. Allocation units are rarely restricted to one type. Many budgets, for example, provide funds for certain formats (e.g., monographs, serials, newspapers, microforms, online information), for individual units of the library (e.g., a branch library, reference department), and for specific subject fields, language groups, or geographic areas. Possible allocation units are listed below:

4.3.1.1. Format. One of the simplest units of allocation is formed by the division into monographs and serials. Other examples of allocation unit by format are memberships, media, microcomputer software, online information, and optical disks.

4.3.1.2. Administrative unit, collection, department, or branch library.

4.3.1.3. Subject. Consider whether broad, specific, or interdisciplinary subject allocations are most appropriate to local needs. Among the determining factors will be the size and type of library and the organization of collection development activity.

4.3.1.4. Method of acquisition (firm order, standing order, approval plan).

4.3.1.5. Discretionary funds, which may include funds for strengthening previously neglected areas, funds for purchases of opportunity, or funds to be held in reserve for emergency needs.

4.3.2. Some budgets include allocation units such as the following to cover expenditures other than those for materials.

4.3.2.1.	Binding
4.3.2.2.	Preservation
4.3.2.3.	Equipment
4.3.2.4.	Other, e.g., bibliographic utilities, shipping, tax.

4.4.   **Selecting allocation criteria**

Allocation criteria may be objective or subjective. Objective criteria are helpful in assuring fairness, but not all factors appropriately considered in the budget process are quantifiable. The following list of allocation criteria is intended to suggest the range of possible factors, rather than present an exhaustive enumeration.

4.4.1.	Current collecting emphasis as described in the collection development policy
4.4.2.	Size and character of the user community
4.4.3.	Need for multiple copies
4.4.4.	Cost of materials
4.4.5.	Amount of relevant publishing
4.4.6.	Extent of reliance on serials, monographs, and other formats
4.4.7.	Need for new information formats and technologies
4.4.8.	Availability of other resources and services in the vicinity
4.4.9.	Potential for external funding
4.4.10.	Statistics on use
4.4.11.	Existence of special gift funds or endowments

4.5.   **Examples of allocation criteria typical of academic libraries**

4.5.1.	Faculty size, composition, scholarly activity
4.5.2.	Undergraduate and graduate enrollment by major
4.5.3.	Credit hours offered by department or academic program
4.5.4.	Degree of dependence of discipline on library resources
4.5.5.	Degrees granted
4.5.6.	Prestige accorded academic or research programs

4.8.1.   Philosophy and goals of the school district

4.8.2.   Intellectual content and level of the collection

4.8.3.   Changes in the curriculum

4.8.4.   Ability levels, learning styles, and social and emotional development of the students

4.8.5.   Attrition rate by loss, weeding, and aging of the collection

4.8.6.   Degree to which the collection includes professional materials for teachers

4.9.   **Application of the allocation criteria: The allocation method**

The allocation criteria chosen will vary according to local needs and will limit the allocation methods that may be appropriately employed. Different methods may assign different weights to the same criteria.

More than one allocation method may be used in different parts of the same budget or be combined in the same part as long as comparable allocation units are subject to the same criteria and methods. Special circumstances, however, such as gifts and exchange programs, special funds, or cooperative agreements, may warrant differential application of allocation criteria. The following allocation methods may be used with a variety of criteria.

4.9.1.   **Historical method**

With this method, the allocations for each new year are based on those of the preceding year, often with an across-the-board increase for each allocation unit. As variants, selected criteria may be applied to selected allocation units (e.g., to allow for the growth of a particular ethnic group or academic department), or differing rates of increase may be applied to different subjects (e.g., a greater percentage increase for science than religion journals). The fundamental division of resources which the historical method embodies, however, is not reexamined each year.

4.9.2.   **Zero-based method**

With this method, the division of resources *is* reconsidered and recalculated each year on the basis of whatever criteria are deemed important. This method takes no account of the allocations of the preceding year. Its sensitivity to change can be both a weakness and a strength, and care should be taken to avoid sudden and drastic changes in allocation due to temporary fluctuations in the criteria used.

4.9.3. Formulas

A formula employs different criteria, which are assigned values or weights, to represent their importance in the allocation process. Using these weights and the raw data discussed above (such as number of majors or users), a numerical value is derived that expresses how much of the total resources budget a given allocation unit should receive. There is no widely accepted formula or generally recognized standard for weighting allocation criteria in formulas. Local needs usually determine the weight given to each criterion. To be effective, a formula must result in a logical and equitable allocation in accord with the criteria selected. The apparent objectivity of formulas can mitigate the political problems often associated with the allocation of scarce resources.

Many believe that the successful application of formulas, however, requires the willingness to deviate from them when appropriate. Critics of formulas claim that such deviations invalidate the formula-based approach. Formulas often prove very difficult to transfer from one type of library to another, or even between comparable institutions. For examples of specific formulas, consult the articles cited in the Selected Bibliography.

4.9.3.1. Ranking

Ranking represents a type of formula-based method of budget allocation. This method involves deciding upon a set of criteria to apply to each allocation unit, assigning numerical values to those criteria, and mathematically translating those values into a raw number. This number is then used to assign a rank order to each allocation unit, and those units with a higher rank receive proportionally greater allocations.

4.9.3.2. Percentages

This method allocates the information resources budget

according to the percentage of the total institutional budget devoted to the subject represented by each allocation unit.

As a variation of this method, different criteria, such as enrollment, size of faculty, circulation activity, and publishing output, are quantified and expressed as percentages. These percentages are then compared for consistency with the equivalent percentages from the information resources budget.

4.9.3.3. Other modelling techniques

In the past, most formulas have dealt with only a limited number of criteria and a limited amount of data. With the widespread availability of microcomputers and the implementation of integrated library systems, including management information systems, there is potential for building dynamic, multi-factor models for resource allocation.

4.10. Review of the budget process

4.10.1. Both allocation criteria and allocation methods should undergo regular review to ensure that they support library goals and plans.

4.10.2. The evaluation of the budget for the previous year, as actually expended, and its comparison with the newly developed budget is an important part of the review process.

4.10.3. De facto allocations, such as ongoing serial costs, should also be subject to regular and continuing analysis.

4.10.4. Once costs of continuing obligations have been forecast or projected, the budgeting officer and others may usefully review current acquisitions strategy, i.e., the combination of methods by which materials are acquired, to determine whether the degree of dependence on each (e.g., subscriptions, approval plans) remains appropriate to existing resources and overall priorities.

4.10.5. When planning to make significant changes in allocation units, criteria, or methods, consider implementing them over time in order to retain some comparability of data between years and promote acceptance of change. Changes in serials commitments and approval plans must occur at an appropriate time in the budget cycle and cannot always be immediately undertaken.

11

5.   **Tools for budgeting**

Data on library programs, information resources costs, and publishing output is essential to the allocation process.

5.1.   **Programmatic information**

Budgets are specific to an institution insofar as they support a particular mission and relate to the needs of a particular clientele. Obtaining information to document those needs is an essential part of the budgeting process. Relevant information sources include:

5.1.1.   **Annual reports by selectors and collection development officers**

Documents that assess the state of the collection and articulate needs for the future can be useful. To the degree that they are objective and factual, they help to indicate the adequacy of current funding. Annual reports often include information on trends such as new programs or demographic changes that enables the budget officer to anticipate future needs.

5.1.2.   **Budget requests**

Budget requests directly address the funding needs for the future year. Typically, they include detailed information on the funds needed in specific areas to support programs.

5.1.3.   **Collection policy statements**

Collection policy statements can provide useful background information on the characteristics of the clientele served, programs supported, and collecting levels by subject.

5.1.4.   **Collection evaluations**

Systematic collection evaluations that identify strengths and weaknesses can assist the budgeting officer in the allocation of resources. To be useful for budgeting purposes, such an evaluation should be followed by a plan that outlines the resources necessary to be allocated over a specified period of time to bring about the desired changes in the collection. The Resources and Technical Services Division's publication *Guide to the Evaluation of Library Collections* (published by the American Library Association in 1989) amplifies on techniques for conducting such evaluations.

5.1.5.   **Characteristics of the population served**

Budgeting officers, selectors, and others should undertake regular assessment of the constituency served in order to keep the emphasis of collection activity consistent with changes in the interests of the user population.

5.1.6.   Use or user studies

Objective data that can confirm or contradict perceptions about the collection and its users may validate or discredit allocation criteria based on assumptions about the user population.

5.1.7.   Cooperative agreements with other institutions

Cooperative collection development agreements with other institutions may be factors in increasing certain allocations while decreasing others.

5.2.   Cost information and publishing output

An important part of the budgeting process is gathering information on costs and maintaining awareness of local as well as national and international cost trends.

5.2.1.   Institution-specific information

5.2.1.1.   Allocations and expenditures from the previous year can provide benchmark data.

5.2.1.2.   Information from circulation and acquisitions systems

Locally generated statistical reports from acquisition and circulation systems can provide valuable management information regarding the growth and use of the collection, and costs of information resources by type, vendor, etc.

5.2.1.3.   Vendor reports

Serials and approval plan vendors often provide institution-specific information on serial cost changes, on relevant monographic publishing output, and on the cost of monographs by country or classification. However, the level of subject detail varies and may not always serve the needs of a specific library.

5.2.2.   External cost information

Factors such as currency exchange rates, inflation, and publishing output may influence budgeting decisions.

5.2.2.1.   Vendor-supplied information about publishing costs in general may be based on materials supplied to institutions having similar characteristics or may apply to a broad spectrum of publishing and institutions. Understanding the scope of such vendor information, when it is not institution-specific, is essential for using that information appropriately.

5.2.2.2. Statistics on prices

A number of publications report average prices of monographs, serials, or other formats by subject and by country of publication. Most of these lists have particular limitations, which the budgeting officer must understand. Some specific sources for price information are listed in the Appendix. The following remarks apply to such sources in general.

5.2.2.2.1. Monographic prices

Several sources issue annual compilations of prices for monographs published in the United States and elsewhere. These compilations tend to be based on trade books and are therefore more relevant to public and school libraries than to academic or special libraries. Other annual listings reflect the particular focus of undergraduate, liberal arts institutions.

5.2.2.2.2. Serial prices

Some listings of serial prices reflect the cost of commercially produced titles rather than academic, small press, or technical titles. As such, the figures are more relevant to public and school libraries than to academic and special libraries. On the other hand, the bias in the price statistics produced by large vendors is toward the kind of titles purchased by the academic and research libraries they serve.

5.2.2.2.3. Foreign titles

Several foreign vendors now furnish statistics showing the average prices of monographs and serials in their own databases.

The Library of Congress for many years has published the average cost of foreign monographs it has purchased.

5.2.2.3. Publishing output

Sources that assess publishing output, by country of origin or by discipline, can aid the budgeting officer in determining the cost of acquiring a specified percentage of that output. Output statistics also document increasing or decreasing rates of publication.

5.2.2.4. Currency exchange rates

Foreign vendors and American vendors dealing with foreign materials are by necessity knowledgeable about the economic factors affecting the prices of foreign materials and are usually willing to share their forecasts on currency fluctuations and inflationary trends with librarians. Additionally, newspapers provide an up-to-date source of information on exchange rates. Library and business journals can be helpful in providing projections and an historical record of the performance of the dollar vis-à-vis other currencies.

GLOSSARY

Allocation: The process of distributing available financial resources at the disposal of an organization for specified purposes and functions. Also, the amount so distributed to subaccounts of the information resources budget.

Allocation unit: A category or subdivision for which a distribution of resources is made; e.g., an administrative or academic department, subject, format.

Budget: A comprehensive financial plan for a given time period, which sets by established categories the estimated expenditures required to accomplish the goals of an organization within the limitations of known or projected income.

Encumbrance: An internal commitment to use funds for a designated purpose. It forms an expression of intent in order to prevent limited funds from being overspent.

Forecast: A prediction of the future economic environment on the basis of various statistics describing past and present conditions. Short-term forecasts can be helpful in constructing the information resources budget.

Information resources: Sources of information in all media, including books, journals, manuscripts, maps, sound recordings, video and electronic formats. Traditionally, most information resources in libraries have been purchased for ownership; funds devoted to information in electronic formats may serve to provide access to such information instead of ownership.

Planning: The administrative or managerial function concerned with the formulation and review of goals, objectives, programs, budgets, policies, procedures, and other types of planning within an organization. The planning function establishes the future directions of the organization, and the resulting plans unify the activities toward agreed-upon results.

Price index: A number used to show the effects of price change on a fixed group of items over a period of time. A price index has a base period of one or more years. The average price in the base period is typically assigned the index value of 100; the average price in succeeding years is divided by the average for the base period, then multiplied by 100 to yield the price index for each year.

Programmatic: Relating to the programs by which the goals and objectives of an organization are realized.

Projection: An economic forecast based on the assumption that the direction and extent of current economic trends will continue into the future.

APPENDIX

SOURCES OF PRICE INFORMATION ABOUT
LIBRARY MATERIALS

Grannis, Chandler. "19--: The Year in Review. Title Output and Prices," *Publishers Weekly,* March issue.

————. "Book Title Output and Prices, Final 19--Figures," *Publishers Weekly,* October issue.

The specific titles of the articles may differ, as will the specific date of the issue in which the indexes appear. The first article gives preliminary figures for calendar year.

Higher Education Prices and Price Indexes: 19-- Update. Washington, D.C.: Research Associates of Washington, September 19--.

Akie, Ronald. "Periodical Prices 19-—19-- Update," *Serials Librarian,* annually in various issues.

Clack, Mary Elizabeth. "Price Index for 19--: U.S. Serial Services," *Library Journal,* April 15, 19--.

Newsletter on Serials Pricing Issues. Marcia Tuttle, ed. Chapel Hill, N.C.: Association for Library Collections & Technical Services, 1989–.

Available electronically through BITNET (contact TUTTLE@UNC.BITNET for further information).

Young, Peter R. and Kathryn Hammell Carpenter. "Price Index for 19--: U.S. Periodicals," *Library Journal,* April 15, 19--.

The specific authors of these indexes vary from year to year.

Soupiset, Kathryn A. "College Book Price Information, 19--," *Choice,* March 19--.

U.S. Library of Congress. "Library of Congress Monograph Receipts for 19--," *LC Information Bulletin.*

This table of receipts, issued at irregular intervals, records numbers of receipts and their average price and may cover more than one year of receipts. This compilation of data has traditionally been published in the *LC Information Bulletin,* but its distribution is under discussion at present.

"Book Trade Research and Statistics," *Bowker Annual of Library and Book Trade Information.* New York: Bowker, 19--.

This section of the *Bowker Annual,* usually issued at mid-year, reports book trade information for the preceding calendar year. It includes ten tables prepared under the auspices of the Association for Library Collections & Technical Services Library Materials Price Index Committee in addition to information adapted from *Publishers Weekly, The Bookseller,* and elsewhere.

The specific articles and indexes include:

"Book Review Media Statistics."

"British Book Production, 19--" adapted from *The Bookseller,* January 19--.

Grannis, Chandler B. "Book Sales Statistics: Highlights from AAP Annual Survey, 19--;" "Book Title Output and Average Prices:19--. Preliminary Figures;" "U.S. Book Exports, Imports, and International Title Output, 19--."

Lenzini, Rebecca T. "Prices of U.S. and Foreign Published Materials."

"Number of Book Outlets in the United States and Canada," adapted from the *American Book Trade Directory.*

In addition to the sources listed above, many vendors provide information about prices and will often prepare data about an individual library's costs over a period of years. Many approval plan dealers, in particular, provide annual cost information regarding the titles treated in their plans for specified periods.

For additional information about sources for prices of foreign materials, see Frederick C. Lynden, "Prices of Foreign Library Materials: A Report," *College and Research Libraries* 49 (May 1988): 217–231. Information about prices for materials in specific subject areas (such as medicine, law, children's books) can be found in the serial literature serving those fields.

BIBLIOGRAPHY

ALLOCATION OF THE INFORMATION
RESOURCES BUDGET

General Studies

Bender, Ann. "Allocation of Funds in Support of Collection Development in Public Libraries." *Library Resources & Technical Services* 23 (Winter 1979): 45–51, esp. 49–50.

Bentley, Stella A., and David Farrell. "Beyond Retrenchment: The Reallocation of a Library Materials Budget." *Journal of Academic Librarianship* 10 (Jan. 1985): 821–825.

Cargill, Jennifer. "Bottom Line Blues: Preparing Library Budgets." *Wilson Library Bulletin* 61 (June 1987): 31–33.

Information Power: Guidelines for School Library Media Programs, 69–84 and 124–130. Chicago: American Library Association, 1988.

Lopez, Joanne Schneider. "The Great Leveler: The Library Budget." The Charleston Conference. *Library Acquisitions: Practice and Theory* 12 (1988): 229–234.

Martin, Murray S. "The Allocation of Money within the Book Budget." In Robert D. Stueart and George B. Miller, eds. *Collection Development in Libraries,* 35–66. Greenwich, Conn.: JAI, 1980.

Packer, Donna. "Acquisitions Allocations: Equity, Politics, and Formulas." *Journal of Academic Librarianship* 14 (Nov. 1988): 276–286.

Schad, Jasper G. "Allocating Materials Budgets in Institutions of Higher Learning." *Journal of Academic Librarianship* 3 (Jan. 1978): 328–332.

―――. "Fairness in Book Fund Allocation." *College & Research Libraries* 48 (Nov. 1987): 479–486.

Sellen, Mary. "Book Budget Formula Allocations: A Review Essay." *Collection Management* 9 (Winter 1987): 13–24.

Senghas, Dorothy C., and Edward A. Warro. "Book Allocations: The Key to a Plan for Collection Development." *Library Acquisitions: Practice and Theory* 6 (1982): 47–54.

Size of Literature Approaches

McGrath, William E. "Determining and Allocating Book Funds for Current Domestic Buying." *College & Research Libraries* 28 (July 1967): 269–272.

McPheron, William. "Quantifying the Allocation of Monograph Funds: An Instance in Practice." *College & Research Libraries* 44 (March 1983): 116–127.

Missineo, Leonard. "Supply-side Measurement: A Formulation for the Allocation of Book Funds in Public Libraries." *Technical Services Quarterly* 2 (Spring/Summer 1985): 61–72.

Welch, Erwin K. "Price Versus Coverage: Calculating the Impact on Collection Development." *Library Resources & Technical Services* 32 (April 1988): 159–163.

Werking, Richard Hume. "Allocating the Academic Library's Book Budget: Historical Perspectives and Current Reflections." *Journal of Academic Librarianship* 14 (July 1988): 140–144.

Usage-based Approaches

Allen, G. G., and Lee Ching Tat. "The Development of an Objective Budget Allocation Procedure for Academic Library Acquisitions." *Libri* 37 (Sept. 1987): 211–221.

Lane, Larraine M. "The Relationship between Loans and In-House Use of Books in Determining a Use-Factor for Budget Allocation." *Library Acquisitions: Practice and Theory* 11 (1987): 95–102.

McGrath, William E. "A Pragmatic Allocation Formula for Academic and Public Libraries with a Test for Its Effectiveness." *College & Research Libraries* 34 (May 1973): 219–222.

Pierce, Thomas J. "An Empirical Approach to the Allocation of the University Book Budget." *Collection Management* 2 (Spring 1978): 39–58.

Schmitz-Veitin, Gerhard. "Literature Use as a Measure for Funds Allocation." *Library Acquisitions: Practice and Theory* 8 (1984): 267–274.

Formula Approaches

Genaway, David C. "PBA: Percentage Based Allocation for Acquisitions." *Library Acquisitions: Practice and Theory* 10 (1986): 287–292.

———. "The Q Formula: The Flexible Formula for Library Acquisitions in Relation to the FTE Driven Formula." *Library Acquisitions: Practice and Theory* 10 (1986): 293–306.

Mulliner, Kent. "The Acquisitions Allocation Formula at Ohio University." *Library Acquisitions: Practice and Theory* 10 (1986): 315–327.

Shirk, Gary M. "Allocating Formulas for Budgeting Library Materials: Science or Procedure?" *Collection Management* 6 (Fall-Winter 1984): 37–47.

Sweetman, Peter, and Paul Wiedemann. "Developing a Library Book-Fund Allocation Formula." *Journal of Academic Librarianship* 6 (Nov. 1980): 260–276.